I'M STILL IN HERE

JAN MATTHEWS GARDNER

ISBN 979-8-88851-794-9 (Paperback)
ISBN 979-8-88851-795-6 (Digital)

Covenant Books
11661 Hwy 707
Murrells Inlet, SC 29576
www.covenantbooks.com

To my Creator, whose strength and love carry me when I feel no one else can.

To my husband, who meant it when he said, "For better or worse."

To my family and friends, who encourage, support, and understand my daily struggles.

To Dr. David Charney, who suggested I write this.

To my late father, Frank J. Matthews.

And finally, to all who are faced with living life with brain injury.

You are not alone, and you are stronger than you think.

I'M STILL IN HERE

Have you ever had a near-death experience? The Mayan calendar predicted the end date of a 5,126-year-long cycle in the Mesoamerican Long Count calendar to be December 21, 2012. Many people interpreted this to indicate the world would end on that date. Tragic behavior ensued, ranging from people giving away all their worldly goods in anticipation of a one-way trip to a better place to cults leading members into mass suicide. As we all know, December 21, 2012, came and went quietly and uneventfully, if not somewhat abashedly. For me, though, it actually was a done deal as my world had already come to an end on December 12, 2012.

Weeks would pass before we would know the full story, and months before the vast spectrum of the destruction my body had suffered. But on December 12, 2012, I was overdosed due to a hospital accident via IV-administered Dilaudid during a garden-variety gallbladder attack. As a result, I was mostly dead, long enough to sustain an anoxic brain injury (ABI) that caused two lesions on my brain. The brain injury left me permanently disabled and unable to continue working a job at which I had invested nearly twenty years and was about to realize my dream promotion. Since the hospital had neither condescended to inform us that the overdose could have caused serious damage, nor to conduct brain scans themselves at the time and had merely indicated I was fine—who wouldn't be after having no respiration for over four minutes and requiring two rounds of Narcan? And as I knew who I was and where I was and recognized my husband, we were later sent on our way without so much as a word of warning. I had two strikes against me at the outset: a stubborn distrust of doctors and the fact that our home and the hospital are located in Virginia, a decidedly nonplaintiff state with a very short bar date in medical malpractice cases.

Accordingly, it would be months before we understood the full ramifications of my brain injury: precious long-term memories gone forever, the inability to consistently convert short-term to long-term memories, aphasia, PTSD, and worst of all, the inability to organically fall asleep. Nor would I find legal recourse, as if any amount of money could ever be considered sufficient for the death of my "self."

My life after beginning my second marriage had seen me become a confident and determined career-oriented woman who could read arduous and complex patent law changes and condense them to their most salient points for the convenience of the attorneys employed at the intellectual property (IP) firm where I worked. Devising and supervising the implementation of new procedures were practically part of my DNA. I was a consummate multitasker and was known to answer emails from overseas clients from my hospital bed. The firm had flown me overseas for a two-day trip so that I could walk an important client through patent rule changes and how we were implementing new firm procedures to accommodate the same.

I rode a commuter train to work, essentially commuting the hours of a part-time job to get to my full-time job. At last, my hours and hours of overtime and effort had paid off. I had ridden the merry-go-round for nearly twenty years and was about to grasp the brass ring when the calliope music stopped. Suddenly, I was faced with finding a new way of seeing myself and living. For the first time, as a long-married couple, my husband was now the sole income provider. His second career as a certified financial planner (CFP) was going well and would continue to grow and prosper. After spending twenty-seven years as a law enforcement officer, his pension was definitely a blessing. As for myself, being accustomed to making a six-figure income, the comparable pittance awarded to me by social security disability was hard to swallow. Who and what was I now?

Our children were grown and on their own, even beginning to have children of their own. I had lost my primary purpose and had to find myself a new one. Having lived with well-controlled depression for years, I knew the alternative, and returning to that dark place was not something with which I could live. My late father, Frank Jackson Matthews, carried a flamethrower during the battle of Iwo Jima at the age of eighteen and was the only man in his platoon to survive.[1] His blood runs through my veins, and as a Matthews, giving up was not an option.

There would be heavy days when the peace of death would seem inviting, if for no other reason than to get to sleep. When I found myself seriously considering how best to legally take my leave of this world with the least amount of inconvenience to my loved ones, those loved ones would somehow show up and, in sometimes loud and painfully raw confrontations, would pull from me the caustic anger turned inward that is depression. I am a Christian and believe these events were not random in nature, but one of the many times, my Creator would catch and hold me in His hands until I could follow him out of the dark again. One of the hardest parts of having this type of brain injury in my case is that I am aware of the difference in myself in real time. It's maddening to struggle to find words and to be told you are repeating yourself. Living with brain injury is one of the hardest things a person can do, but I am a survivor of other traumas that most people will thankfully never have to endure. So I fight on, knowing that somehow, somewhere, I'm still in here.

The journey to our discovery that I had suffered a serious brain injury began when I doggedly attempted to return to work. I had suffered a bowel obstruction due to adhesions—apparently, my maternal family line is predisposed to this problem—which was, in my opinion, poorly handled by the hospitalist surgeon who, for some reason, decided to fully cut me open midline when it could have been done laparoscopically. Three weeks to the day after having that surgery, I was back in the hospital with my own new surgeon, who had to reopen the midline incision and correct some "mechanical" issues. Translation: doctors cover for each other's mistakes.

After being released from the hospital yet again, I eventually had the thirty-two or so staples removed and, minus several feet of intestine, headed into the office. En route to the office, my already shell-shocked husband had to stop me from jumping into morning rush hour traffic as I began to experience pain beyond anything I had ever endured, including childbirth. What I assumed to be yet another bowel obstruction turned out to be a gallbladder attack.

After a false start at a different but closely located hospital, we ended up back at my least favorite place on earth, where my surgeon correctly diagnosed the problem and ordered me placed on an intravenous pain pump to administer Dilaudid while we prayed the gallstone stuck in my bile duct would back out and I would not have to be cut open yet again. It was far too soon since my midline surgeries to allow the removal to be done laparoscopically. The stone did indeed back out of the duct, sparing me from being cut open. Unfortunately, for unknown reasons, the pain pump administered too much Dilaudid, and I had nearly left this world when night nurses' assistants randomly came in to check my vitals only to discover that I was no longer breathing and my heart was about to stop. Since my husband had stayed with me in my hospital room and was dozing in the luxurious recliner provided for family members, who wish to remain with their loved ones, he was to have a front-row seat to my near-death experience. His twenty-seven years on the police force served him well when the aids were unable to wake me or to elicit any response from my ice-cold body. He immediately jumped on top of me and vigorously shook me while screaming that I could not leave him. Codes were called, and again by the grace of God, the crash cart with the Narcan was just across the hall. My husband was unceremoniously removed from me and watched as a highly competent and calm nurse rode point on the administration of two rounds of Narcan, finally bringing me back to the land of the living.

I have no memory of any of this though my husband will never forget it. What I can attest to is that as I awoke in the morning, I noticed every muscle in my body ached. I then realized I could not move. Over ten pounds of blankets had been piled on me. My husband, with a death grip on the bed rail, while staring at me with bloodshot eyes, asked, "Do you remember anything?" I believe I attempted to flippantly reply that while I could not remember anything after dinner the previous night, I felt as though I must have escaped the confines of the hospital and been in a bar fight. He didn't laugh. Thus, I survived death nine days before the world was supposed to end, but I survived not as myself. I didn't know what was ahead of me, and looking back, I sincerely appreciate the mercy of not knowing my life would, for a time, become a film noir.

Again, I was eventually released from the hospital and returned to work, thinking my greatest challenge would be to will myself not to have another gallbladder attack until the surgery to remove my stone-filled organ could be performed laparoscopically. I would return to my high-pressure job with the aplomb of any Matthews. Though I physically resemble my late mother to an uncanny degree, I am in absolutely every other way my father's daughter—not prone to panic or fear nor one to admit defeat easily. The only problem was I had not noticed that the calliope music had stopped.

Back at the office, I was trying to return to a routine. I had just read an impressively hefty and well-written internal manual regarding new patent law and firm procedures. A colleague was in my office when I commented on the quality of the document and asked who had written it. As I looked up into her perplexed face, she answered me, "You wrote that." I had absolutely no memory of the subject of the manual, much less having written it. Thus, my first indication that something was very wrong finally stung me, but instead of leaving an irritating itch, I was touched by the cold electric shock of something I had not felt for years—anxiety.

I casually wondered whether I should be worried but was determined to will myself to recover and move on with my life. Sometimes, a strong will is a wonderful and powerful thing. This would not prove to be such an occasion as my job and my life began to unravel with increasing speed, and I realized will alone would not save me. I did make it to the required date when my gallbladder could be removed laparoscopically and had that done with no complications. This time, I was out for significantly less time before I once again returned to work.

After spending time back at the office, I knew there was a serious problem. I no longer remembered subjects in which I had been well-versed. Memos I had clearly written carried my name but no familiarity. My colleagues noticed I had become *feistier* when dealing with recalcitrant Associates. If I'm honest, I have never had a high tolerance for stupid people. My patience was sorely tested daily, and though I had tried to function at my pre-injury level and hold a steady course, the inevitable day came when my boss called me into his office. In a perfunctory and brief conversation, I was informed there had been a change of plans and I would not be receiving the promotion. Suffice it to say, I felt sucker punched and betrayed. My late father used to say, "Everyone has a point"—a line in the sand. And at that moment, I reached mine.

Calmly returning to my office and shutting the door, I quickly boxed up my most personal things and called my husband.

"Remember when I said I would ride this roller coaster until I couldn't do it anymore?" I asked him. He didn't get an opportunity to reply before I followed with "That day is here. Come and get me."

I then prepared and signed a simple and succinct notice of resignation letter, placed it in an inner-office envelope to be delivered by the end of the day, gathered up my things, and waited in my office for my husband to arrive. He called me when he was downstairs in front of the building, and I quickly and quietly carried my things down the stairs and left the building. When I got into the car, we agreed that I would find a neurologist and get a handle on my health. If I could go back in time, I would have gone to a neurologist right away. When it comes to anoxic brain injuries, my standing rule now is to trust no one. Continue to seek answers, speak with your doctors, and make use of Brain Injury Association resources until you are satisfied you have been fully informed.

I am told some people have problems collecting social security disability. Having previously gathered my medical records for a non-start lawsuit, I found it to be a fairly simple process. We submitted the requisite paperwork and records, and in due course, I was called to come in to be interviewed and tested by a government nurse. In very short order, I was declared to be fully and permanently disabled due to an anoxic brain injury. I would never be able to reliably turn short-term memory into long-term memory. The precious old memories I lost would never be fully recovered. I would not be able to learn new skills although I have managed to learn that someone with an ABI requires roughly five times the energy to accomplish any task as someone with a fully functioning brain.

Less than a month later, I received a disability check covering the period of time back to the established onset date of the ABI. It was official—I was 100 percent disabled to the point that my husband is now the designated guardian of whatever small amount of money I do collect. I married a damn saint. My husband is my guardian, my rock, my comfort, and on occasion, the person plucking my very last nerve (I never said he was perfect.) For someone who had graduated from high school a year early at age sixteen and had been considered focused, extremely smart, and capable, this news was a punch in the gut but also a relief. I have never feared death and do not understand people who want to live long lives. Even as a child, I could never visualize myself as an old person. Now that I knew I was not going insane, the one thing I do fear, I could take a breath. Becoming accustomed to the new limited version of me took some work, is a work in progress. After over ten years, I'm still discovering who I am now. Early in the process, my Creator began to surprise me with what I have come to call my *parting gifts*. It's best to laugh.

We took a trip to visit a son and his family for Halloween in upstate New York. Wanting to surprise me, my husband booked a luxury suite on the Canadian side of Niagara Falls. The hotel contained a casino, and as we walked past the roulette tables, I casually stopped to watch the spinning wheels. Neither of us being gamblers, my husband saw the minimum buy-in and declined to waste the money. I asked to remain for a moment and that he observe me as I would guess red or black. A few moments later, he regretted his initial decision as I had correctly called each spin of the wheel. We left the hotel to take our grandchildren trick-or-treating. It was cold and damp and perfect. No, I have not become a career gambler guided by some mysterious part of my brain activated when another part of my brain died. It is sometimes fun to imagine such a scenario though I can no longer tolerate large and loud crowds. My Creator knows my limitations.

• • ○ • • •

SOMETHING STUPID
THIS WAY COMES

I am no stranger to trauma. One reason for the abundance of adhesions in my abdomen is the number of times I have had to undergo emergency surgery requiring midline incisions—five as of this time. Several of those are the result of bowel obstructions. Two of those instances, however, are the result of childbirth-related complications. In fact, the first midline incision I had was done because I had suffered a complete abruption of the fetal placenta during the birth of my second-born son. The pregnancy had been as textbook and uneventful as that of my older son; and while I went into labor at thirty-eight weeks—for those who don't know—thirty-eight-to-forty week gestation is still considered full term. At the hospital, I expected to receive a quick epidermal and to deliver a baby so fast he would have jet lag as had happened with my first son. Instead, when I felt my water break, the nurse checked me, and immediately, the whole world went into warp speed. What I had assumed was amniotic fluid was in fact blood. The placenta had completely separated from my uterine wall, and my baby was suffocating inside me. I was also bleeding out though I can't say that even registered with me. I was wheeled into a delivery room for an emergency C-section where I was cut open midline to save precious time.

Having received an epidural, I was awake, if not yet completely numbed. When my son was removed from my body, he was not breathing. The operating room staff worked on him and did revive him though he never made a sound. I was sewn and stapled up and put in a recovery room. Calls were made, and family members began the journey to our hospital. Later, the doctor arrived to tell me that my son was in stable but critical condition. However, every part of his brain had been damaged due to the lack of oxygen, and he would therefore be profoundly disabled. In all likelihood, he would be deaf, blind, and mute. It was too soon to tell the extent of his injuries, but I began to mentally prepare myself to be the mother of a special-needs child.

I sent my husband to rent an electric breast pump because it was anticipated that my son would not have the ability to swallow. As a firm believer that breastfed is best fed, I saw no reason to delay this process. A church friend who happened to be the father of a young man who had been born with cerebral palsy came to visit, and it was shortly afterward that I first saw my son. He was peacefully asleep in the neonatal intensive care unit (NICU). I was not allowed to hold him at that time, but I saw him and that was enough. My son was alive, and I had a purpose—a purpose to proceed with all that was necessary to care for him. However, the next morning, the doctor came into my room, and as my late mother stood beside my bed, he began to verbally tap-dance around a subject. I have always had a highly developed b.s. detector. I immediately focused on him like a laser and firmly asked him, "What are you trying to tell me?" "This baby is going to die within the next fifteen minutes," he replied.

My late mother, in her typical fashion, immediately became a useless jumble of nerves. I demanded to be taken to my son, and after dialing the phone for my now nearly catatonic mother, I rather tersely instructed her to get my husband back to the hospital. I was then taken by wheelchair to the NICU where, for the first time, I was permitted to hold my beautiful son as he died. All I could do was tell him how much I loved him and how sorry I was this was happening. All I could see was his perfect face—eyes still closed, never having seen anything or anyone in this world—as the monitors displayed his rapidly deteriorating vitals. Mercifully, the NICU had been cleared of other parents, and shortly after his father arrived, my sweet son left this world without ever having made a sound. The doctor removed the ventilator tube and turned off the machines and allowed me to continue to cherish my son. Eventually, the fatigue of the surgery and my psychological exhaustion drove me to permit them to take Jordan out of my arms, and I was returned to my room. Before permitting anything else to be done for me, I issued instructions for his funeral. Only then would I accept the medications to dry up my milk and rest.

When a child dies, which is in no way the natural order for the human species, it can evoke strange behavior in people. For me, although my son had lived outside my body for only just over two days, I had already seen his entire life in my head, and I had loved him fiercely for the entire time I carried him inside my womb. I would not even consider the doctor's recommendation that I remain in the hospital. There was nothing else I would ever be able to do as his mother, so I called the local newspaper for the obituary I had written, dispatched my mother to purchase the clothes in which to bury him, left the hospital, was driven to the funeral home and planned, and later attended Jordan's funeral and his burial. The service was conducted at our church, and he was buried in the same local cemetery where his father's family who had predeceased him were buried. It was then that I learned some people become utterly full of stupidity on such occasions. A close friend indicated that he couldn't bring himself to attend the funeral because it was just too difficult for him. A family member could not understand why I wasn't immediately over my loss because my son wasn't a real baby, having lived such a short time. If you take nothing else from this, please know that it is *always* best to simply say, "I am so sorry, I just don't know what to say," than to say something stupid, regardless of how well-meaning your intentions may be. Sadly, the hurtful remarks were not lost during my brain injury.

The entire experience was one of such pain, despair, anger, and irrationality that at one point, I remember shaking my fist at the heavens and crying out to God Almighty, "Who the hell do you think you are?"

At the time, it made perfectly sane sense to me. I vowed that if I ever returned to speaking terms with Him, my first question to God if and when I finally met him would be "Why?" I know now that no explanation could ever suffice. It took me a very long time to learn to live with the grief and pain of losing my son, and I will never be able to say I completely have overcome that loss. The death of a child never ceases to hurt; one must learn to live with the pain. Let me simply say that in the movie *Steel Magnolias*, Sally Field's character absolutely nails it. I still can't watch the funeral scene without crying. As I said earlier, I have survived trauma most people will never know. The process of recovering from tragedy is not one with which I am unfamiliar. This ability and faith in my Creator, who is tough enough to accept my anger as well as loving enough to overlook my outburst, combined with the love and support of my family, has been everything to me as I am learning to live with my new self. It is a continuously ongoing process that does, on occasion, include surprises. I still stand by my contention that a simple "I'm so very sorry" will always be better received than uninformed and hurtful assumptions and remarks.

Recently, I was on the receiving end of such a verbal assault when told that due to my brain injury, I was thought to be unstable and irrational. It was a pathetic and deliberate attempt to provoke or hurt me made by a bully who should know better. To paraphrase another line from *Steel Magnolias*, if you can't say anything nice, *go away*. I simply will not waste my precious limited energy and resources to idly suffer the folly of fools. You know who you are.

• • ◦ • •

IT'S THE MOST WONDERFUL TIME OF THE YEAR

Since there does not exist a *cloud* against which a person can reconcile their memories, discovering that a cherished memory is gone is most often made especially gutting—pun intended—because it occurs when loved ones are together for a holiday and reminiscing about the past. It was during our first holiday season together as a family after the overdose that I was asked by our grown children to tell the story of a particular Christmas that illustrated perfectly how our blended family initially more resembled the Addams Family than the Brady Bunch. I could not accommodate the request because I possessed no such memory. Others quickly jumped in, and the story was told. But to me, it was just that—a story. I felt like any outsider hearing an amusing anecdote. Those really deep belly laughs have been taken from me.

We have learned that holidays, birthdays, and other special occasions are the times when someone will most likely bring up something from our shared past and I will learn about something that occurred in my past while utterly devoid of the emotions associated with having been there. Memory is a strange thing. In my case, I have come to know that most anything associated with music is more likely to have survived. Anyone who wasn't fortunate enough to have a father, who beautifully played Debussy's "Clair de Lune" on the piano while the females in the home completed their ablutions prior to an outing, has my sympathy. Of course, anything associated with extreme anger or pain also seems to be similarly stored in multiple areas of my brain. Any married men reading this should now be offering my husband *their* sympathy.

During a vacation to the Smokey Mountains, we discovered another one of God's *parting gifts*. After a day of hiking in the park, we went to visit family who live in the area. As the unofficial family genealogist, I had been painfully processing information into our family tree. Since I can literally read an ancestor's name at the top of a page and forget it by the time I've scrolled to the bottom of the page, this is a cumbersome process. A writing instrument was needed, and when I found none inside, I went outside to their jeep to retrieve a pencil. My cousin and husband were on the deck grilling, and his wife was in the kitchen cooking when they noticed a black bear standing next to the side of the jeep opposite to me. Calling me by my full first and middle names (an action to be taken in only the most extreme situations) my cousin told me to come inside. I and, for that matter, the bear ignored him.

A few seconds later, my cousin's wife quietly entered the carport and, in a low tone, said, "I don't want you to be scared, but there is a bear about four feet away from you."

I literally felt absolutely no fear, only mild curiosity as I glanced around and replied, "Oh, really? Where?"

At that point, she physically took me by the arm and led me back into their home. And thus, I discovered that I no longer possess a fight-or-flight reaction to large wild animals of whom I perhaps should be fearful. Judging by the bear's behavior that day, as well as on subsequent occasions, animals feel no threat from me and are thus just as uninterested as one can be without being completely rude. Some people feel this is not a gift. I feel such people are to be pitied. I don't suggest anyone should ever get between a mother animal and her young (of any species); however, I was raised to respect but not fear wildlife. After an ABI left a couple of holes in my brain, my subconscious finally got the message.

• • ◦ • •

PERCHANCE TO DREAM

The National Organization for Rare Disorders (NORD) says that fatal familial insomnia (FFI) is a rare genetic degenerative brain disorder. It is characterized by an inability to sleep (insomnia) that may be initially mild but progressively worsens, leading to significant physical and mental deterioration. Similar to other prion diseases, the disease is invariably fatal. Life expectancy ranges from seven months to six years, with an average of eighteen months.[2]

I do not suffer from this disorder. However, like many people with brain injuries, I have lost the ability to organically fall asleep. Initially, my insomnia was not horrible. I could read until my eyes were tired and I would fall asleep. I maintained strict "clean sleep hygiene" by religiously following a routine like turning off the television, avoiding caffeine, and doing everything by the book. I added melatonin supplements as the insomnia grew worse and increased in frequency. Inevitably, there came a point where it was intolerable. Being sleep deprived and having an ABI is a cascading and exponentially worsening situation. I quickly found it essential to speak to my general practitioner.

The sleep aids prescribed had no effect. I sought further help, eventually ending up, out of desperation, in a local urgent care facility. There I was prescribed the first of two one-off medications that would be tried on me. By one-off, I mean medications intended for other purposes, such as a psychotropic drug that were given to me in doses that would knock out a grown man in a full psychotic break. Initially, I was grateful for anything that would allow me to fall asleep. A short time later, the side effects kicked in, starting with weight gain and including a particularly cruel twist with one medication that allowed me to fall asleep. But if I was awakened at any point in the night thereafter, I was up for the day. It was during the particular year I caught the flu, then mononucleosis, and was finally left anemic that I was referred to a new doctor to monitor my blood levels.

After collecting my medical history, she recommended an alternative one-off medication that would allow me to wean off the psychotropic medication and would have much less in the way of side effects. It was a hellish process and took months to accomplish, but I finally was off the psychotropic drug. Getting my strength back, I even felt motivated to enroll in an exercise class and looked forward to the scale soon registering lower numbers. I enjoyed the class taught in a small facility with plenty of breathing space. The hard exercise contributed to my ability to fall asleep. It was just what I needed right up until the day I ripped open a small vertical hernia I have just at my xiphoid process. A small section of the intestine popped out of me with only slightly more alarming effects than when the embryonic xenomorph first popped out of the character Kane's chest in the movie *Aliens*.

Fortunately, I was able to lie flat, force myself to relax, and using two knuckles of my fist, push the escaped intestine back inside. This had happened to me under other circumstances before a few times, but this time it continued to hurt a lot worse. After consulting my doctor, it was decided that for safety's sake—safety being the avoidance of more surgery—I could no longer engage in the core challenging exercises. So I confine myself to hiking, my elliptical machine, and simple stretching exercises on a bar my husband installed for me in our recreation room. I was disappointed but determined to regain my strength and pushed on, looking forward to better days and blissful sleep-filled nights. As if.

Once again, my body displayed a positively vulgar level of disloyalty; and despite everything, I continued to gain weight. Having been quite underweight at the start and also being blessed with above-average height, nobody was particularly bothered by this except myself. My husband contends that while he lives to eat, I eat to live. When symptoms of menopause accompanied a nearly comical increase in the size of my bust, my doctor explained to me that the process of weaning off the psychotropic drug at such a high dose had caused my hormones to reset themselves. When I mentioned that I was not losing the weight, she casually noted that the new one-off medication, while much less of a burden to my body, would, at the requisite doses to allow me to sleep, also cause me to continue to gain weight. So there it was—menopause 2.0—and still gain weight if I wanted to avoid insomnia. At this point, I knew I would have to be my own hero in this saga, and hitting the internet, I searched for alternatives. It was there on a day of no memorable import other than that of my discovery that I learned *why* I could no longer fall asleep organically—my brain is missing the section that regulates how my body produces a protein called orexin. This protein regulates the ability to fall asleep as it essentially orders your body to stay awake. I note that none of my doctors had ever informed me of this process. I reasoned that there must surely be a medication that would tell your body when not to produce orexin and again hit the computer.

It was on a day that I will remember better than my own birthday—seriously though, I can't remember the date—that I found there were two fairly new, in the pharmaceutical sense, medications that were specifically designed to treat my type of insomnia. Both are orexin receptor antagonists and armed with this information I spoke with my psychiatrist about the possibility of trying this medication to wean me off the other one-off medication while leaving me able to sleep with minimal impact on my body and much less medication. I had started a bio-hormone replacement therapy via the quarterly implant of a hormone pellet to get my hormones under control and hoped that the new medication, combined with my new sublingual custom compounded troches of progesterone, would enable me to wean off the last one-off and sleep.

By the grace of God, my psychiatrist, who had saved my sanity when I was leaving my first marriage, agreed that we would try to do just this and even permitted me to have direct communication with him via text during this experiment. Again, it took some months and some sleepless nights when my body was refusing to let go of the old medication. But a day came when I could take only the prescribed orexin antagonist, my sublingual progesterone, and an older long-term medication I have been on for depression along with my usual supplements, and I *slept*. The first time I slept through the night it had literally been years, but I *slept*.

This time, the Matthews's determination and will served me well. It was one of the greatest feelings of relief in my life.

I HAVE AN ABI, WHAT'S YOUR EXCUSE?

So how do you function as an average human being when you sometimes forget things immediately after hearing, saying, or doing them? You get creative and learn to take preemptive measures in some social situations; to leave visual clues for yourself when taking medication (I have mine separated into morning and evening, and when I take medication, I turn the bottle upside down) and to develop a healthy relationship with the GPS/map application on your phone along with antianxiety breathing.

We have six grandchildren, and our children trust unequivocally that I can safely babysit their children. More importantly, *I* trust myself to babysit. Having one granddaughter living about fifteen minutes away allows my husband and me to serve as backups to our son and daughter-in-law's daycare. As I work on this portion of my story, I am utterly exhausted from spending the day keeping my two-year-old granddaughter. She is staying overnight, and I get to do the same tomorrow. We play together all day upstairs while my husband works in his office downstairs. There was music, dancing, reading, pretend cooking and tasting of holiday pudding, and most of all, major spoiling going on in here today. There was absolutely no television, and without naming names, someone got rocked to sleep for both her morning and afternoon naps and completed both in my arms in the rocking chair. Some qualities *all* grandparents have in common, with or without an ABI.

I may not be able to remember certain things, but knowing how to care for my grandchildren is still intact. Apparently, years and years of having done it once before, ensured memories would become stored in multiple areas of my brain. At least in my case, I remember how to read, write, drive, walk, talk, and many other functions everyone untouched by brain injury takes for granted. Learning new skills has been a crap shoot. My skills as a seamstress have actually improved if I don't try to push through becoming tired. If I am asked to draw something, everyone involved is going to be disappointed. I don't know until I try to do something whether I will be able to accomplish the task. Being fatigued is a real handicap, and my aphasia gets much worse under such circumstances. Aphasia is a causative disorder, and mine was caused by an anoxic brain injury.

According to the National Institute on Deafness and Other Communication Disorders (NIDCD), aphasia is a disorder that results from damage to portions of the brain that are responsible for language. Sometimes, my aphasia causes me to combine and/or create new words, though many are worthy to be added to the English lexicon in my humble opinion.

With the steadfast encouragement and support of fraternal organization sisters, I pushed myself completely out of my comfort zone, a good habit for anyone and one I intend to continue. It's important to remember that building walls to protect yourself from being hurt will also keep anyone from reaching in to help. So I made a commitment to take an office in our fraternity that took everything I had to fulfill. My husband was by my side, and I successfully completed my year in the top office of our fraternal organization.

We make a conscious effort to avoid situations I know will be triggers, such as large, loud crowds. If the space is not too enclosed and I carefully monitor my feelings, I know when to move myself to a safer, quiet space. If I know an event will be more than I can handle, I don't put myself into the situation. Like someone who has overimbibed, my level of inhibitions has been lowered. That doesn't mean I'm easy, but if pushed hard enough, I will reply with all the skills one would expect from a Southern woman and the daughter of a WWII marine. I cannot abide cowardice and will not tolerate bullies. Accordingly, if you are easily shocked by vitriolic rages from the visage of a sixty-four-year-old grandmother, buckle up, buttercup. Most especially when in extreme pain, I will not muzzle myself. Your position or title will afford you no protection. As I once heard Judge Judy say, "I am an ecumenical abuser."

Further, I assure you it is infinitely more frustrating to me than it is to anyone else that an innocuous scent, sight, sound, or word can cause my damaged brain cells to ping around like a vintage pinball, leading to everything from partially recovering an unrelated memory to the incitement of a family riot. There is no point in mincing words. Having this brain injury sucks. I can be as nurturing as any doting grandmother and, when sufficiently angered, as terrifying as anyone's worst nightmare.

Usually, there is no hiding my anger with the usual aplomb of a true Southern woman. The ability to glide like a swan while paddling madly underwater was killed off in me on December 12, 2012. It is worth noting that when provoked, a swan can be fiercely aggressive and painfully effective in attacking. I don't feel at all ashamed that I once drove an emergency room nurse to say she had never in her long career heard such language from a grandmother. Well, sugar, a medical professional caused this brain injury; and if medical professionals have to listen to this grandmother go off on them like a marine drill sergeant, I absolutely refuse to feel guilty. As a matter of fact, my late father once expressed that he was more intimidated by his gunnery sergeant than the Japanese military when he was ordered to remove the flamethrower from the still-warm body of the US Marine who had just been killed by a sniper during the battle of Iwo Jima and to put it on his own 140-pound back. That is the stuff from which I descend—and that is the Matthews will of which I shall always be proud.

So now what? Find the remaining parts of yourself and your life that you want to nurture and grow. If you recognize the parts that you need to jettison, then go ahead and do that too. Sometimes, people in your life, including family, can fall into that category. Your peace and health must be your priority. Forgive and move on as best as you can. When you have experienced severe trauma, your list of priorities becomes forever changed. Things once thought to be important sometimes don't even make the list anymore. I believe that is a healthy response, and as long as I do not feel the sudden need to commit crimes, the people in my life can accept these changes. The people who decided they could no longer be my friend were, I now know, never my friend. That's another of the worst parts of having a brain injury; that is the stuff that really hurts. I've mourned the loss of friends over these last ten or more years. I never get used to that feeling and believe that too is actually a healthy quality in me.

I FEEL YOUR PAIN

My late maternal grandmother used to say that I "took on colors." This old Southern expression refers to someone who is highly empathetic and will begin to feel what others are feeling. One would think this is a wonderful quality right until one begins to experience it. Apparently, my ABI somehow enhanced this ability in me, to the point that I literally have to mentally say "Shields up" in some instances. I have also become somewhat of a human lie detector. If you see me looking at you with my left eyebrow slightly raised and my head tilted, you should know it's likely I am questioning your veracity or your choice of apparel.

When I was young and my body still intact, I could look at my children in such a manner, and they would usually end up confessing to a multitude of sins. Every mother possesses the *look* that holds their child bound like prey locked in a cobra's stare and compels them to tell the truth. Mine is simply much more effective now. I can feel a liar from a distance and have no patience with them. It all goes back to my intolerance for cowardice. A liar is too frightened to tell the truth and is therefore, in my opinion, a coward.

There will be people in your life who will never be able to handle someone with an ABI. Driven by ignorance or lack of empathy, some people will behave as though this disability is not truly a disability. Such people are not worth my time, and I will let them know it right before I cut them from my life with the cool precision of a surgeon. I don't know why people believe you must keep toxic people in your life because of an accident of genetics. Family or friend, if you bring nothing to the table but poison, yours will be a very brief stay at said table. Even if you don't have a brain injury, nobody should ever tolerate being abused in any sense of the word. Perhaps my tolerance for such behavior has taken a dive due to this brain injury, but I have long believed a person can only take so many *hits* before they realize they have reached their limit. I now have a clear understanding of my limit. My limit was profoundly changed on December 12, 2012. Further, I am now acutely aware of my responsibilities to take care of myself and that I alone control how I respond in any given situation. Words are nothing more than sounds and only carry as much importance as we assign to them. Trust is now a precious commodity, and mine must be earned.

• • •○• • •

WAYS I COPE WITH MY ABI

Remember, if you've seen one brain injury you've seen one brain injury. These hints are things I find helpful. Other people may feel differently.

Keep multiple calendars. I have one printed paper calendar and also use my phone calendar.

Get your medication in order, separate morning and evening. When you take your dosage, turn the bottle upside down, or use some other visual clue.

When getting low on medication, leave yourself a visual clue. I set it out on the bathroom counter turned upside down. I also apply this to any items kept in our bathroom. Obviously, the main bedroom and bathroom are safely gated off when grandchildren are present.

If I remember something at an odd time, I either mention it to my husband or write it down or both.

Prioritize your health at all times. If I get overly tired, I will pay for it. A sleep-deprived person with a brain injury is neither desirable nor particularly safe.

Tell your doctor what is working *and* what is not working. You cannot assume the doctor knows about anything. Maybe they do, but if it is something new or unusual, they may not. If you don't feel your doctor is helping you, then move yourself to a different doctor. Most states have brain injury associations; avail yourself of their resources. The sleep medication I take has to be ordered because so few people use it.

Medical professionals are humans and therefore not omniscient. Be your own advocate. Ask questions and take notes. If you are not satisfied with a hospitalist surgeon or other doctor if you are in an emergency department, demand your own, call them yourself, or ask for the administration personnel tasked with handling these issues in the hospital.

Always keep a list of your medications and dosages with you, especially when you travel. I always carry my medications in my carry-on luggage and *never* check them when traveling by air. I have never been questioned by the TSA.

Update or have an attorney prepare an advance life directive to ensure your wishes will be respected should you become incapacitated. Personally, I have a standing do-not-resuscitate order (DNR). I do not want to be resuscitated if my heart stops. Some people feel differently and that is perfectly fair.

If you need a moment to respond to something, take your time. People who know me understand this, and it generally isn't a problem. You have nothing for which you need to apologize. Occasionally, I remind people that I did not do this to myself and to please refrain from interrupting me.

Because of my spotty short-term memory problems and being legally disabled, I obtained a handicapped parking permit through my doctor and the Department of Motor Vehicles (DMV). Knowing I will always be able to find my car is a great relief. It only took one time of my having to walk all over a parking lot while pressing my key fob for a good hour for me to make this a priority.

Push against your limits if you can. My ancestry genealogy hobby is as much to force myself to try to go further as it is to find interesting ancestors. I have learned to use my cell phone camera instead of writing things down now.

Listen to your body. If it is saying rest, then rest. Recent ancillary health issues have made day trips particularly taxing for me. I am therefore extremely judicious in scheduling them. In my case, if I must attend something that is going to entail a day trip, I make sure I have a day of complete rest following the trip.

Try to find purpose for each day. I enjoy cooking holiday meals and new recipes. I tried several new recipes for Easter dinner this year and learned that next time I will need to have a helper for the particular meal I prepared. I have also started upcycling and repurposing items. My husband has patiently taught me how to use his power tools, and I find working with wood to be particularly soothing.

Consistent *clean* bedtime hygiene is essential, even with effective sleep medications.

Avoid morning appointments if possible. I may not always be able to fall asleep at a decent hour, and now I require more sleep than prior to the brain injury.

Don't give up! Yes, there will still be crappy days. There will also be beautiful days. Helping others always makes me feel better.

ENDNOTES

[1] Murphy, Alisa. 2015. *You Don't Know Jack*. Charleston, South Carolina, CreateSpace KDP.

[2] https://rarediseases.org/rare-diseases/fatal-familial-insomnia/

[3] Me with my late father at a Marine Corps Birthday Ball

ABOUT THE AUTHOR

Jan Matthews Gardner is a unique blend of someone born in the Deep South, raised in California, and is ultimately completing her own circle by ending up in rural Virginia. She makes her home in Virginia with her husband and four large rescue dogs. A lover of history, genealogy, and skills no longer easily found, Gardner is the daughter of a WWII marine and considers it her duty to push on against all odds, as did her father during the Battle of Iwo Jima.

* 9 7 9 8 8 8 8 5 1 7 9 4 9 *